TONGA MAP

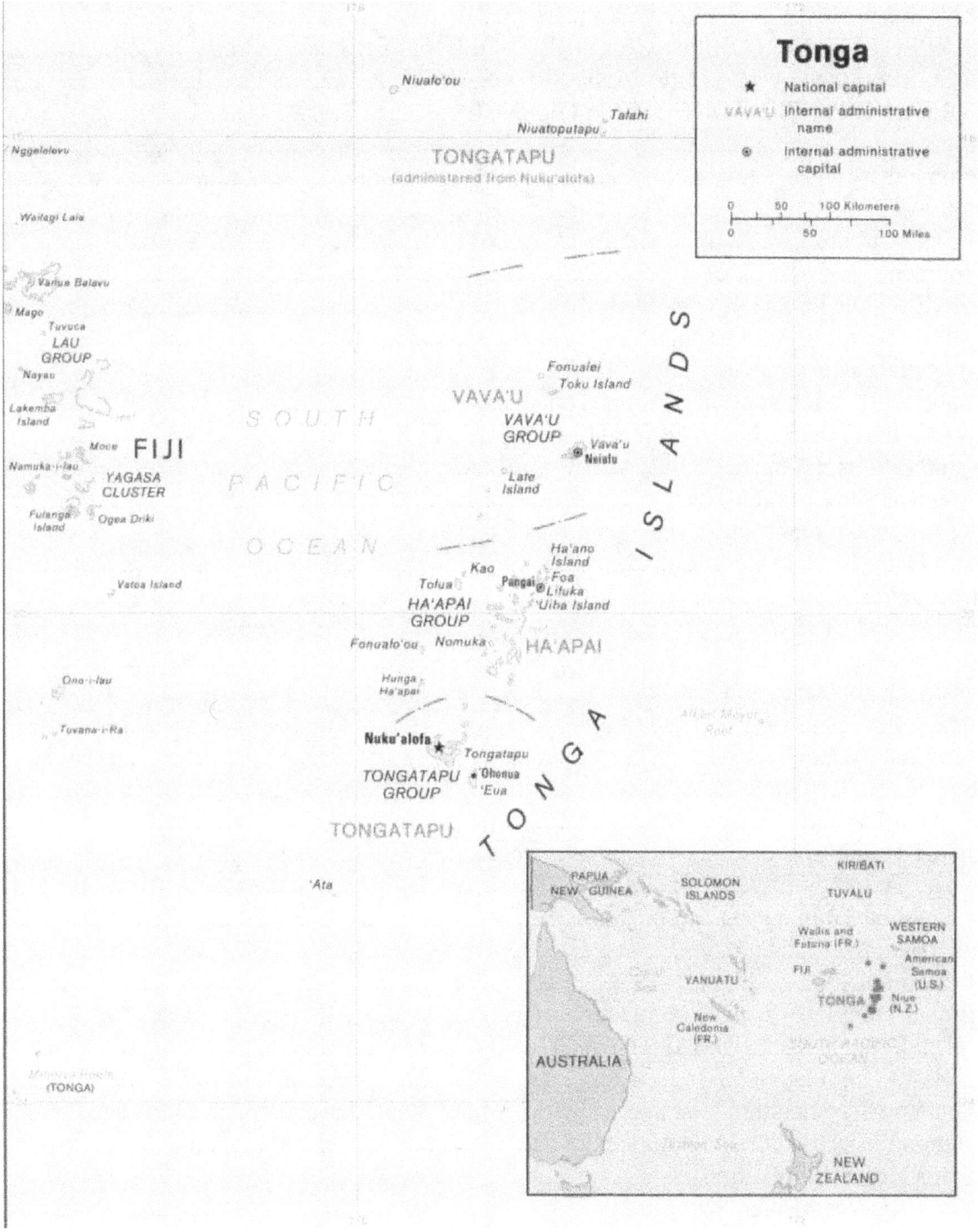

Tonga

★ National capital

VAVA'U Internal administrative name

⊙ Internal administrative capital

Niualo'ou

Talahi

Niuatoputapu

TONGATAPU
(administered from Nuku'alofa)

Nggelelevu

Waitagi Lala

Vanua Balavu

Mago

Tuvuca

LAU
GROUP

Nayau

Lakemba
Island

Moce

FIJI

Namuka-i-lau

YAGASA
CLUSTER

Fulanga
Island

Ogea Driki

Vatoa Island

Ono-i-lau

Tuvana-i-Ra

SOUTH

PACIFIC

OCEAN

Fonualei

Toku Island

VAVA'U

VAVA'U
GROUP

Vava'u
Neiafu

Late
Island

Ha'ano
Island

Kao

Foa
Pangai
Lifuka

Tofua

Uiha Island

HA'APAI
GROUP

Fonualo'ou

Nomuka

HA'APAI

Hunga
Ha'apai

ISLANDS

Allan Mayer
Reef

Nuku'alofa ★

Tongatapu

TONGATAPU
GROUP

Ohonua

'Eua

TONGATAPU

TONGA

'Ata

Minerva Reefs
(TONGA)

0   50   100 Kilometers

0   50   100 Miles

KIRIBATI

PAPUA
NEW GUINEA

SOLOMON
ISLANDS

TUVALU

Wallis and
Futuna (FR.)

WESTERN
SAMOA

American
Samoa
(U.S.)

FIJI

VANUATU

TONGA

Niue
(N.Z.)

New
Caledonia
(FR.)

SOUTH PACIFIC
OCEAN

AUSTRALIA

Tasman Sea

NEW
ZEALAND

CONTENTS

CORE EXPECTATIONS
FOR PEACE CORPS VOLUNTEERS

In working toward fulfilling the Peace Corps Mission of promoting world peace and friendship, as a trainee and Volunteer, you are expected to:

1. Prepare your personal and professional life to make a commitment to serve abroad for a full term of 27 months

2. Commit to improving the quality of life of the people with whom you live and work; and, in doing so, share your skills, adapt them, and learn new skills as needed

3. Serve where the Peace Corps asks you to go, under conditions of hardship, if necessary, and with the flexibility needed for effective service

4. Recognize that your successful and sustainable development work is based on the local trust and confidence you build by living in, and respectfully integrating yourself into, your host community and culture

5) Recognize that you are responsible 24 hours a day, 7 days a week for your personal conduct and professional performance

6. Engage with host country partners in a spirit of cooperation, mutual learning, and respect

7. Work within the rules and regulations of the Peace Corps and the local and national laws of the country where you serve

8. Exercise judgment and personal responsibility to protect your health, safety, and well-being and that of others

9. Recognize that you will be perceived, in your host country and community, as a representative of the people, cultures, values, and traditions of the United States of America

10. Represent responsively the people, cultures, values, and traditions of your host country and community to people in the United States both during and following your service

PEACE CORPS/TONGA
HISTORY AND PROGRAMS

History of the Peace Corps in Tonga
Peace Corps Volunteers have served in the Kingdom of Tonga since October 1967. King Taufa'ahau Tupou IV invited their entry and from the initial group of 39 Volunteers, more than 400 Volunteers and trainees were in the Kingdom within one year's time. The Volunteers in these early intakes were primarily engaged in teaching in primary and secondary schools throughout the country. However, the Volunteers came from a variety of educational and work backgrounds and offered their technical knowledge to build capacity in agriculture and fisheries, public health, architecture and construction, environment, business and cooperatives, and youth development.

In 1982, a major country review and evaluation recommended that the Peace Corps focus on more technical assistance to government ministries and sponsoring organizations. For the rest of the decade, Volunteers focused their efforts on teaching science and vocational education at church schools. Half of the Volunteers worked with government agencies in fishing and agriculture where they helped identify local Tongans for boat ownership, trained local fishermen in deep sea fishing techniques, and taught business skills. During this time, some Volunteers also began working in health cooperatives, in the mass media, and in energy-related areas.

A country evaluation carried out in 1989 recommended that the size of the program was too large. Thus, program size was decreased to around 50 Volunteers annually, where it remained for the rest of the 1990s. In 1992, primary teacher trainers were reintroduced to Tonga. They were assigned to primary schools as teacher trainers and to the Curriculum Development Unit of the Ministry of Education to help teachers improve their methods of bilingual classroom instruction.

In the mid-1990s, Volunteers began serving as secondary school teachers in biology, chemistry, and physics, while others continued to teach English as part of a new national literacy curriculum at the primary school level. During this time, the program expanded to include Volunteers working in economic development to build capacity in accounting and business advisory, environment with a focus on environmental education, renewable energy, the development of habitats and national parks, and youth development.

Volunteers continued working with unemployed and at-risk Tongan youth as sports instructors, small business and vocational skills advisors, and environmental educators at the community level into the early 2000s. During this time, Volunteers also focused on organizing youth groups and mobilizing them to start community service projects and community computer centers.

In the mid-2000s, Peace Corps/Tonga introduced the business and organizational development (BOD) and community education (CE) projects that incorporated elements from previous programs, including the community-based youth development project, the community microenterprise development project, and the business educational development project. Volunteers in the community education project worked with counterparts as teacher trainers at the primary school level to build their capacity in new teaching methodologies and resource development, while Volunteers in the business and organizational development project sought to build the capacity of government ministries, nongovernmental organizations (NGOs), and service providers, and of entrepreneurs and community members in information technology, accounting, and other business practices.

A single Tonga Expanded Community Education Project (TECEP) plan started in 2009. It focused on both formal and informal education at the village and town levels. Volunteers provided direct instruction in English language, business education, industrial arts, teacher training, and information and communications technology (ICT) to primary, secondary, and tertiary school students. Volunteers also co-planned and team-taught, when possible, with current school teachers. Volunteers acted as resource developers for the schools in which they served. They designed appropriate instructional materials and organized extracurricular activities that reinforce learning. This role beyond the formal classroom is where Volunteers worked as catalysts of informal education, service learning, and community development activities in the village. This approach helped establish schools as centers for community education and development throughout Tonga.

In 2012, there is yet another change to the program in Tonga. Peace Corps/Tonga is initiating a primary-level teaching English as a foreign language (TEFL) program. This change is in response to a need for more focused technical training. In addition to TEFL, Volunteers will be expected to initiate other projects during their service, such as healthy living projects, community clean-up and other environmental tasks, computer instruction, and other efforts that depend on personal interests and skills.

Historically, over 1,500 Volunteers have worked in more than 30 areas of development sponsored by the Tongan government, private nonprofit organizations, and individual communities.

COUNTRY OVERVIEW:
TONGA AT A GLANCE

History

It is widely accepted that around 3000 BC, an Austronesian-speaking population known by archaeologists as the Lapita people migrated into the Pacific from Southeast Asia and were the early ancestors of today's Polynesians. In 2007, archaeologists confirmed the first settlement of the Lapita people in the entire Pacific in the village of Nukuleka on Tongatapu. Around 2000 BC, the Lapita people abandoned their initial settlements and voyaged to the farthest eastern reaches of Polynesia.

Around 500 BC, a second wave of voyagers, now known as Polynesians, settled the Tongan archipelago on their long migration across the South Pacific. Around AD 950, according to a myth, the supreme Polynesian god known as Tangaloa came down to Tongatapu and fathered a son by a lovely Tongan maiden. Their son, Aho'eitu, thus became the first Tui Tonga—king of Tonga—and launched one of the world's longest-running dynasties. The dynasty first ruled from the village of Toloa and then from the present-day village of Niutoua, the home of the Ha'amonga _a Maui Trilithon.

Moving the capital to Lapaha on the shore of the island's interior lagoon about 800 years ago, they took advantage of a safer anchorage for the large, double-hulled war canoes. These were used to extend their empire as far as Rotuma and the Lau island group in Fiji, Tokopia in the Solomon Islands, present day Wallis and Futuna, Niue, and Samoa. At that time, a deep passage linked the lagoon to the sea; it has been slowly closing as geological forces raise the island and reduce the entrance to the present shallow bank.

Dutch navigators in 1616 were the first Europeans to view the Tongan archipelago. The main island of Tongatapu was first visited by the Dutch explorer Abel Tasman in 1643. Continual contact with Europeans, however, did not begin until more than 125 years later. Captain James Cook visited the islands in 1773 and 1777 and during his voyage in 1777 he was hosted on Lifuka by a powerful chief named Finau I. Cook was so impressed by this show of hospitality that he named the Ha'apai group "The Friendly Islands," the modern kingdom's motto. Unbeknownst to Cook, however, Finau I and his chiefs apparently plotted to murder him and his crew, but they couldn't agree among themselves how to do it before the great explorer sailed away.

Captain Bligh and HMS *Bounty* visited Lifuka in 1789 after gathering breadfruit in Tahiti. Before he could leave Tongan waters, however, the famous mutiny took place near the island of Nomuka in the Ha'apai group.

Some 20 years later, Chief Finau II of Lifuka captured a British ship named the *Port au Prince,* stealing all of its muskets and ammunition, setting it on fire, and brutally slaughtering all but one member of its crew. The survivor was a 15-year-old Londoner named Will Mariner. He became a favorite of the chief, spent several years living among the Tongans, and later wrote a four-volume account of his experiences. He told how the Tongans mistook 12,000 silver coins on the *Port au Prince* for gaming pieces they called *pa'angas.* The national currency today is known as the pa'anga.

The arrival of Wesleyan missionaries on Lifuka in the 1820s coincided with the rise of Taufa'ahau, a powerful chief who converted to Christianity in 1831. With their help, he won a series of domestic wars. By 1845, he had conquered all of Tonga and declared himself to be the new Tui Tonga.

Taufa'ahau took a Christian name and became King George I of Tonga. In 1862 he made his subordinate chiefs "nobles," but he also freed the commoners from forced labor and instituted the policy of granting each adult male a garden plot in the countryside and a house lot in town. He created a Privy Council of his own choosing and established a legislative assembly made up of representatives of the nobles and commoners. This system was committed to writing in the Constitution of 1875, which still is in effect today. The assembly is known now as Parliament.

King George I died in 1893 at the age of 97, thus ending a reign of 48 years. His great-grandson, King George II, ruled for the next 25 years and is best remembered for signing a treaty with Great Britain in 1900, which turned Tonga's foreign affairs over to the British and prevented any further encroachments on Tonga by the Western colonial powers. Consequently, the Kingdom of Tonga was never colonized.

King George II was succeeded in 1918 by his daughter, the 6-foot-2 Queen Salote (her name is the Tongan transliteration of Charlotte). For the next 47 years, Queen Salote carefully protected her people from Western influence, even to the extent of not allowing a modern hotel to be built in the kingdom. She did, however, come to the world's attention in 1953, when she rode bareheaded in the cold, torrential rain that drenched the coronation parade of Queen Elizabeth II in London (she was merely following Tongan custom of showing respect to royalty by appearing uncovered in their presence). She later hosted Queen Elizabeth II and Prince Philip in Nuku'alofa.

Queen Salote died in 1965 and was succeeded by her son, King Taufa'ahau Tupou IV. Then in his late 40s, he set about bringing Tonga into the modern world. On the pretext of accommodating the important guests invited to his elaborate coronation scheduled for July 4, 1967, the International Dateline Hotel was built on Nuku'alofa's waterfront, and Fua'amotu Airport on Tongatapu was upgraded to handle jet aircraft. Tourism had arrived, albeit modestly.

In 2005, Tonga's civil servants went on strike demanding better pay. The protest went on for six weeks until the government agreed to raise wages by as much as 60 percent. A year later, a pro-democracy gathering turned into a riot that burned several square blocks of downtown Nuku'alofa.

Following his father's death in 2006 and his coronation in 2008, George Tupou V announced that he would relinquish authority, leading to Tonga's first democratic elections for Parliament in 2010. King George Tupou V is known for this accomplishment and won international praise for bringing democracy to Tonga. He passed away in March, 2012 in Hong Kong.

Crown Prince Tupouto'a Lavaka Ata will take the throne of the island nation following the sudden death of his brother. He is known as King Tupou VI.

Government

Since the adoption of its constitution in 1875, Tonga has been ruled by a monarch whose heirs are entitled to perpetual succession to the throne. The government consists of an executive branch headed by a Privy Council, the unicameral Legislative Assembly (or Parliament), and the Judiciary. The Privy Council assists the king in the discharge of his functions and is the highest executive authority. It is composed of the king, the cabinet, and the governors of Ha'apai and Vava'u. The cabinet of 12 ministers is appointed by the king.

The Legislative Assembly consists of the king's cabinet, nine representatives elected by the 33 hereditary nobles, and seventeen representatives elected by popular vote. Elections for the Legislative Assembly are held every three years. Before democratic reform in 2010, only nine representatives were elected by the people.

The Judiciary consists of a Supreme Court (whose judges are appointed by the king), a Land Court, and a Magistrate's Court, with a right of appeal to a Court of Appeal in respect to land cases, civil cases, and sentences in criminal cases.

The past two decades have been a time of great change in Tonga, especially with regard to its international status. Tonga became a member of the Pacific Forum and the Pacific Conference, both important regional bodies. In 1975, Tonga developed economic and political ties with the European Economic Community with a variety of African, Caribbean, and Pacific nations. It became a full member of the United Nations in 2000, as well as a member of the World Trade Organization in 2007. The most obvious benefit to Tonga from its widening association with other countries has been the inflow of foreign aid from developed countries and international agencies. This aid has enabled the kingdom to improve social services and construct essential infrastructure.

Economy

Agriculture and fishing are the mainstays of the Tongan economy. The main agricultural products are various types of taro, yams, cassavas, sweet potatoes, potatoes, and such fruits and vegetables as bananas, watermelons, papayas, pineapples, mangoes, tomatoes, carrots, and cucumbers. The main cash crops are kava and vanilla beans. Recently, sea cucumber has become a major export to Asia.

Remittances from Tongans living abroad have played a significant role in the economy over the past few decades. The major imports are textiles, building materials, petroleum products, vehicles, and food items.

People and Culture

Tongans have a well-developed sense of community based on a close-knit extended family unit and a close affiliation to their church. Members of Tongan families take care of one another almost unconditionally. One's immediate family includes grandparents, uncles, aunts, and cousins. In many cases, the entire family works together to plant, harvest, cook, and fish. Children typically live with parents or grandparents after marriage. It is quite uncommon for single adult children to live independently of their families.

Religion is woven into almost every aspect of daily life. Tongans attend church regularly and bless each meal, meeting, and event with a prayer. Devoutly Christian, almost all Tongans belong to one of the 20 or so denominations in Tonga. About 43 percent of the population belongs to the Free Wesleyan Church of Tonga, followed by the Church of Jesus Christ of Latter-day Saints (Mormon), the Roman Catholic Church, the Free Church of Tonga, and the Church of Tonga. Laws concerning the Sabbath are strictly upheld in Tonga, and virtually everything closes on Sundays, except for emergency facilities, bakeries (in the afternoon), and some tourist facilities.

Many elements of Tonga's rich traditional culture are still prevalent today, including the wearing of the *ta'ovala*, a decorative woven mat that is tied around the waist. There are certain ta'ovala or *kiekie* (for women) for each occasion, determined by the nature of the work one does and one's social status. Volunteers are usually given a ta'ovala by their host families, and wearing one in professional and religious settings earns Volunteers the respect of community members. In most work settings, you are expected to wear culturally appropriate clothing, especially at government ministries, in places of business, and in the classroom.

Another traditional element of Tongan culture that is still celebrated today is dance, which can be traced as far back as the 15th century. No celebration in Tonga is complete without some form of dancing, and impromptu dances are common to Tonga and other islands in the Pacific. The love of dancing gave rise to a custom called *fakapale*, or giving appreciation for artistry and performance. In modern times, the custom has expanded to include money tucked into a performer's costume, stuck to his or her legs or arms, or placed at his or her feet. Volunteers often participate in or observe Tongan dancing in their communities.

Environment

Tonga has seven official protected areas, including marine parks and national marine and coastal reserves. Unfortunately, conservation is not a high priority in Tonga and funds are limited. Most of its land has been converted into either plantations or town tracts; however, large areas of rain forest and bush land exist on the Niuas and 'Eua, as well as on Tonga's volcanic islands. Along with the forest crater on Tofua, the forest reserve on 'Eua represents the only significant first-growth rain forest in the country.

The most common plant you will see in Tonga is the coconut palm, the ―tree of life" for all South Pacific peoples. The islands' beaches and reefs are home to numerous species of fish, starfish, crabs, and other shellfish. Porpoises, sharks, sea turtles, and migrating humpback whales can be seen in the waters around Tonga. The only land mammal native to Tonga is the flying fox.

RESOURCES FOR FURTHER INFORMATION

Following is a list of websites for additional information about the Peace Corps and Tonga and to connect you to returned Volunteers and other invitees. Please keep in mind that although we try to make sure all these links are active and current, we cannot guarantee it. If you do not have access to the Internet, visit your local library. Libraries offer free Internet usage and often let you print information to take home.

A note of caution: As you surf the Internet, be aware that you may find bulletin boards and chat rooms in which people are free to express opinions about the Peace Corps based on their own experience, including comments by those who were unhappy with their choice to serve in the Peace Corps. These opinions are not those of the Peace Corps or the U.S. government, and we hope you will keep in mind that no two people experience their service in the same way.

General Information About Tonga

www.countrywatch.com/
On this site, you can learn anything from what time it is in Nuku'alofa to how to convert from the dollar to the Tongan currency. Just click on Tonga and go from there.

www.lonelyplanet.com/destinations
Visit this site for general travel advice about almost any country in the world.

www.state.gov
The State Department's website issues background notes periodically about countries around the world. Find Tonga and learn more about its social and political history. You can also go to the site's international travel section to check on conditions that may affect your safety.

www.psr.keele.ac.uk/official.htm
This includes links to all the official sites for governments worldwide.

www.geography.about.com/library/maps/blindex.htm
This online world atlas includes maps and geographical information, and each country page contains links to other sites, such as the Library of Congress, that contain comprehensive historical, social, and political background.

www.cyberschoolbus.un.org/infonation/info.asp
This United Nations site allows you to search for statistical information for member states of the U.N.

www.worldinformation.com
This site provides an additional source of current and historical information about countries around the world.

Connect With Returned Volunteers
and Other Invitees

www.rpcv.org
This is the site of the National Peace Corps Association, made up of returned Volunteers. On this site you can find links to all the Web pages of the ―Friends of" groups for most countries of service, comprised of former Volunteers who served in those countries. There are also regional groups that frequently get together for social events and local volunteer activities.

www.Peace CorpsWorldwide.org

This site is hosted by a group of returned Volunteer writers. It is a monthly online publication of essays and Volunteer accounts of their Peace Corps service.

Online Articles/Current News Sites About Tonga

www.tongatapu.net.to

"Tonga on the 'Net" contains cultural information, stories, history, etc.

http://www.tongaholiday.com/

The Tonga Visitors' Bureau website provides general information, maps, pictures, and samples of traditional Tongan singing.

www.tongastar.com/

The site of the *Tonga Star* (in English and Tongan).

www.nomoa.com/index.php

Current news and links about Tonga by Tongans.

http://www.matangitonga.to/article/global_index.shtml

Current news about Tonga by Tongans.

International Development Sites About Tonga

www.ausaid.gov.au/

Australia's international aid agency.

www.c-spodp.org/Canada_Pacific/CanadaFund.htm

Canada Fund in the Pacific.

www.nzaid.govt.nz/programmes/c-tonga.html

New Zealand Agency for International Development.

www.usaid.gov/

U.S. Agency for International Development.

www.undp.org/

United Nations Development Programme.

www.sprep.org

South Pacific Regional Environment Programme.

Books About the History of the Peace Corps

1.   Hoffman, Elizabeth Cobbs. *All You Need is Love: The Peace Corps and the Spirit of the 1960s*. Cambridge, Mass.: Harvard University Press, 2000.

2.   Rice, Gerald T. *The Bold Experiment: JFK's Peace Corps*. Notre Dame, Ind.: University of Notre Dame Press, 1985.

3.   Stossel, Scott. *Sarge: The Life and Times of Sargent Shriver*. Washington, D.C.: Smithsonian Institution Press, 2004.

4.   Meisler, Stanley. *When the World Calls: The Inside Story of the Peace Corps and its First 50 Years*. Boston, Mass.: Beacon Press, 2011.

Books on the Volunteer Experience

1.   Dirlam, Sharon. *Beyond Siberia: Two Years in a Forgotten Place*. Santa Barbara, Calif.: McSeas Books, 2004.

2.   Casebolt, Marjorie DeMoss. *Margarita: A Guatemalan Peace Corps Experience*. Gig Harbor, Wash.: Red Apple Publishing, 2000.

3.   Erdman, Sarah. *Nine Hills to Nambonkaha: Two Years in the Heart of an African Village*. New York, N.Y.: Picador, 2003.

4.   Hessler, Peter. *River Town: Two Years on the Yangtze*. New York, N.Y.: Perennial, 2001.

5.   Kennedy, Geraldine ed. *From the Center of the Earth: Stories out of the Peace Corps*. Santa Monica, Calif.: Clover Park Press, 1991.

6.   Thompsen, Moritz. *Living Poor: A Peace Corps Chronicle*. Seattle, Wash.: University of Washington Press, 1997 (reprint).

LIVING CONDITIONS AND VOLUNTEER LIFESTYLE

Communications

Few countries in the world offer the level of mail service considered normal in the United States. Mail usually takes a minimum of two weeks to arrive in Tonga and some mail may simply not arrive. Fortunately this is not a frequent occurrence, but it does happen. This is not meant to discourage you, but to prepare you for the realities of international mail service in the South Pacific. Despite the delays, we encourage you to write to your family regularly and to develop a way of tracking letters—such as numbering them. Family members typically become worried when they do not hear from you, so it is a good idea to advise them that mail service is sporadic and that they should not worry if they do not receive your letters regularly. Besides, unless you are on an outer island, you will have regular access to email.

Volunteers who serve on Tongatapu, Tonga's main island, collect their mail from the Peace Corps office. Mail to Volunteers on outer islands is received at the Peace Corps office and forwarded to the islands via the local airline or the local ferry service once a week. Mail for Volunteers living in Vava'u, Ha'apai, and _Eua can be sent directly to the post offices located on those islands. Postal addresses for all post offices are provided upon arrival in-country. During your first six months of service, you will be able to receive packages sent from overseas without paying customs duties.

Your specific address during service will depend on your site location, which is determined during the training process. The main Peace Corps office in Nuku'alofa has a P.O. box for Volunteer mail (U.S. Peace Corps, P.O. Box 147, Nuku'alofa, Tonga, South Pacific), and P.O. boxes have been established on certain outer island groups. Once you know your site location, you can advise your family and friends about the appropriate address to use.

Telephones

Calling the United States from Tonga is expensive and U.S. telephones attached to a service provider like Sprint or Verizon do not work in Tonga. To call the U.S. from Tonga, Volunteers must purchase Tongan telephone cards locally from either the service provider TCC or Digicel. Skype is becoming popular at many Internet cafes around the capital city of Nuku'alofa.

Friends and family in the U.S. may call Volunteers. Most Volunteers do not have land-line phones, but Peace Corps will provide you with a cellphone upon arrival to Tonga. Some Volunteers choose to bring —unlocked" cellphones with them from the U.S. There is no charge for incoming calls on mobile phones and there is no monthly fee. Credit for cellphones (—pay as you go") can be purchased at almost any small shop throughout the kingdom, even in places where there is no electricity.

Computer, Internet, and Email Access

Many Volunteers choose to bring personal laptops to Tonga and are happy with their decision to do so. However, if you are thinking about bringing a laptop, please consider the following: Peace Corps/Tonga cannot guarantee the safety of your computer or replace it if it is damaged or stolen. Tonga's humid climate, ants, and dusty conditions can be hard on electronics. Internet service is widely available in Internet cafes through the main islands of Tongatapu and Vava'u, but it expensive to have Internet access installed in your home and the power supply experiences frequent surges. There are two computers with Internet access at Peace Corps/Tonga's main office in the capital city of Nuku'alofa.

Many of you might be thinking of creating websites or blogs as a way to communicate with your family and friends. If you are thinking of using this type of communication, you must speak with your country director first, as there is some very specific information you need to know before you get started.

Housing and Site Location

Volunteers' host organizations are responsible for identifying and providing safe and suitable housing in accordance with the Peace Corps' criteria. Housing ranges from a one-room *fale Tonga* (traditional hut) with a thatched roof to a two- or three-bedroom wooden or cinder block house with very basic furniture. Peace Corps/Tonga asks host agencies to provide private bath and toilet facilities; however, occasionally Volunteers may have to share facilities with a neighbor.

As access to electricity, running water, and other amenities varies widely, you will need to be flexible. Some Volunteers have electric lights and outlets, flush toilets, and running water in their homes. Others spend evenings reading by kerosene lamp or candle, use a pit latrine, and collect water from a rain tank near their homes.

The Peace Corps will provide you with a kerosene lamp, a life vest, a bike helmet (if necessary), and an AM/FM radio. Once you become a Volunteer, you will receive a settling-in allowance to purchase additional household necessities.

Peace Corps staff members make site visits to Volunteers to provide ongoing support and to follow up on any housing or safety issues that arise. However, Volunteers are encouraged to contact staff if there are any safety-related improvements needed for their homes.

Living Allowance and Money Management

As a Peace Corps Volunteer in Tonga, you will receive various allowances. The living allowance is intended to cover the cost of food, utilities, household supplies, clothing, recreation and entertainment, transportation, communication, reading materials, and other incidentals. It is reviewed at least once a year through a market survey to ensure that it is adequate. Currently, the living allowance is $722 *pa'anga* (TOP), roughly equivalent to $450 (U.S.). The living allowance is deposited monthly into your Peace Corps' bank account in Tonga in local currency.

A vacation allowance of $24 (U.S.) per month, converted into local currency, is added to your monthly living allowance. Also, toward the end of pre-service training, a one-time settling-in allowance of T$1,050, roughly equivalent to US$650, will be deposited into your account to buy basic household items when you move to your site.

If the Peace Corps requests you to travel, you will be given additional money for transportation and meals. The amount is established by the director of management and operations, based on the local cost of transportation and lodging.

Most Volunteers find they can live comfortably in Tonga with these allowances. While many Volunteers bring their own funds to Tonga to cover the cost of travel during vacations, we strongly discourage you from supplementing your income with money from home. You are expected to live at the same economic level as your neighbors and colleagues.

Credit cards can be used in a few establishments in the capital and are useful for vacations and overseas travel. Traveler's checks and personal checks can be cashed at a local bank for a small fee, but there are few retail establishments in Tonga that accept them. Peace Corps/Tonga will assist you in establishing a local bank account.

Food and Diet

Tongan meals consist of staple foods, such as yam, taro, sweet potato, cassava, fish, pork, and canned meats. A common traditional dish is meat or fish wrapped in taro leaves with coconut cream. On Sundays and for special occasions, Tongan families prepare an underground oven called an *'umu*.

Tongan food is generally considered bland by American standards. Root crops are boiled, baked, or fried and often served with salt at every meal. Onions, garlic, curry powder, soy sauce, and chili peppers are usually available, but are only occasionally used in food preparation.

Your diet will vary depending on your site and personal preferences. In the capital and the few other city centers and ports, you will find a reasonable variety of imported foods at grocery stores and a good assortment of locally grown foods at the market. Bread, rolls, pastries, and ice cream are readily available through commercial operations and family-run shops in the city centers, but often unavailable in remote villages and outer islands. Noodles, flour, sugar, rice, eggs, butter, milk, canned fish, meat, seasonal fruits, and a few basic vegetables are available in most small shops on the main islands. The living allowance is sufficient to buy some imported fresh and canned fruits and vegetables to take to remote sites.

The main meats are pork, chicken, and mutton, but shops in the capital also sell beef, hamburgers, sausages, and hot dogs. Fresh fish can be purchased from markets and local fishermen throughout Tonga. Tropical fruits grow on most islands, but availability of particular items varies by the season. Tongans do not eat many vegetables, so some Volunteers choose to plant and maintain vegetable gardens in their communities. Canned foods, such as fish, corned beef, and processed snacks, are readily available and both locals and Volunteers eat these regularly.

It is possible to maintain a vegetarian diet in Tonga, but it can be difficult at times. Root crops and some leafy-green vegetables are available year-round. The few other vegetables grown locally are seasonal and supply varies depending on your location. There is a wide variety of fruits in Tonga, though many are also seasonal. Papayas and bananas are available year-round. Finding alternate sources of protein may present an ongoing challenge, especially for Volunteers on outer islands.

Being a vegetarian in Tonga may present a few cultural challenges, as well. A meal without meat is considered incomplete and inadequate by Tongan standards. This makes it difficult to explain why one would choose a vegetarian diet. When living with or visiting Tongan families, you will be offered traditional foods; Volunteers are encouraged to try local cuisine out of respect for their hosts.

Visitors usually eat only with selected members of the family, with children eating in a different place. It is common practice in Tonga to eat with your hands. However, eating and drinking while standing or walking is not considered appropriate, even though you may see others doing this.

Transportation

Volunteers may bring bicycles from home or buy them locally. Distances are not great in Tonga, and the low traffic density is conducive to travel by bike. Peace Corps/Tonga issues helmets to Volunteers who own bicycles or you may bring your own. If a Volunteer brings a bike from the United States, he or she is responsible for the transportation costs (usually airline fees) from the Volunteer's home of record to Tonga.

Local buses and taxis run on Tongatapu, Ha'apai, and Vava'u and tend to be reasonably priced. Travel among islands is by air, boat, or both. Chathams Pacific Airline has regular flights from the main island to the other major islands of Tonga and inter-island ferries provide service to outer islands, large and small, throughout Tonga.

For safety reasons, Peace Corps/Tonga prohibits Volunteers from owning, driving, or riding on motorcycles and from owning or driving private cars for any reason. Violation of these policies may result in the termination of your Volunteer service.

Geography and Climate

The Kingdom of Tonga consists of 171 islands, 36 of which are inhabited, and is spread over 144,000 square miles (360,000 square kilometers) of ocean. The total land area is only 268 square miles (670 square kilometers), about the size of Memphis, Tennessee. About 77 percent of the total land area is arable—the highest percentage in the world. The highest point in the island groups is Kao, which rises to over 3,300 feet (1,000 meters).

Tonga lies west of the international date line, which was bent to include Tonga in the same time zone as its neighbors. For this reason, Tonga is one of the first countries in the world to welcome each new day.

The islands of Tonga were formed on top of two parallel submarine ridges. Between the two ridges is the shallow Tofua Trough, which is 31 miles (50 kilometers) wide. Along the western ridge are many volcanoes, most of which are dormant. Kao, Late, Fonualei, and Tafahi are the remains of cones formed after violent volcanic eruptions millions of years ago. The ocean west of these ridges is known as the Tonga Trench. It is 1,860 miles (3,000 kilometers) long and 62 miles (100 kilometers) wide and extends from Samoa to the southeast of New Zealand. At one point the trench descends to 35,617 feet (10,793 meters), the second deepest trench in the Pacific Ocean.

‘Eua, on the eastern ridge, is one of the oldest islands in the Pacific. ‘Eua has steep cliffs on its eastern side and is home to the last remaining rain forests in Tonga.

Tonga's climate is mild to warm, humid, and moderately wet. Although the temperature varies little, there are distinct wet and dry seasons. The wet season, which also brings cyclones, is from November to April, with average temperatures of 77 to 81 degrees Fahrenheit. The dry season is from May to October, with temperatures of 71 F to 75 F (at night, it can get as cool as 60 degrees). The climate of northern Tonga (e.g., Niuatoputapu and Niuafo'ou) is about 5 degrees hotter than the rest of Tonga and has more rainfall.

Social Activities

Tongans are very social and enjoy team sports. Rugby is the national sport, and most villages also have competitions in volleyball, basketball, table tennis, soccer, and tennis, which are almost exclusively male sports. Women play netball, field hockey, and sometimes volleyball and soccer. Movies, videos, card games, and dances are also major forms of recreation. Men gather to drink kava root juice, converse, and sing late into the night. Families have picnics on the beach for special occasions, and feasting is an appropriate way to celebrate anything, and everything, in Tonga.

Men traditionally build boats, canoes, and houses and are proficient in woodcarving. Women traditionally weave mats and baskets and make *tapa* (cloth made of the bark of the mulberry tree), dolls, and flower necklaces.

Professionalism, Dress, and Behavior

Modesty is very important in Tonga and Tongans take pride in their appearance. By law, Tongan men over age 16 must wear shirts in public places, and many do not even take off their shirts in their own homes. Most Tongan women do not wear short skirts, sleeveless tops, or low-necked dresses outside their homes. Pants are not considered appropriate for women in certain areas. Except when worn as athletic wear or while working in the garden, shorts are considered improper on women, especially outside the capital. However, shorts may be appropriate as swimwear, and women do wear them at home and in public under wraparound skirts.

Please review the packing list carefully. Volunteers often bring clothes to Tonga that are too casual for their work assignment. Men are expected to dress similar to their male counterparts at school, in the office where they are assigned, or in the village. This often means wearing a *tupenu* (wraparound cloth skirt), *ta'ovala* (mat worn around the waist), and ironed shirts with collars. Sometimes, even wearing a tie and suit jacket is appropriate.

Likewise, women are expected to dress like their female counterparts at the schools, in the offices where they are assigned, or in the villages. This typically means wearing long dresses, skirts (that come down to at least midcalf), and tops that provide modest coverage. Sleeveless shirts are never appropriate, nor are short dresses. However, it is possible to purchase long wrap skirts to wear underneath short dresses. Tongan women frequently do this when their skirt or dress is not long enough by cultural standards. Wearing T-shirts is never appropriate for your work assignment, though you may certainly wear T-shirts inside your house.

You also will need black clothing during your service in Tonga. Black is generally the prevailing color seen throughout the village and the city and is always appropriate. Black clothing is especially important if there is a formal event, such as a funeral, that you must attend. Also, Volunteers should be prepared to wear black clothing for funerals.

Black *tupenus,* a traditional wraparound skirt, or pants and black collared shirts for men are appropriate. All male Volunteers will purchase tupenus here in Tonga, as will most female Volunteers. Long, solid black dresses or skirts with a black blouse or jacket are appropriate for women.

To gain the acceptance, respect, and confidence of community members and colleagues, it is essential that you dress and conduct yourself professionally. The Peace Corps expects you to behave in a way that will foster respect toward you in your community and reflect well on the Peace Corps and on the United States. You will receive an orientation about appropriate behavior and cultural sensitivity during pre-service training. As a Volunteer, you have the status of an invited guest and, thus, must be sensitive to the habits, tastes, and taboos of your hosts. Behavior that jeopardizes the Peace Corps' mission in Tonga or your personal safety may lead to a decision by the Peace Corps to terminate your service. Refer to the *Volunteer Handbook* for more information about the grounds for administrative separation. In the words of a Volunteer, "Dressing appropriately and speaking Tongan are the easiest ways to gain the respect of the Tongans. These two things can make the difference between getting by and thriving."

Personal Safety

More detailed information about the Peace Corps' approach to safety is contained in the —Health Care and Safety" chapter, but it is an important issue and cannot be overemphasized. As stated in the *Volunteer Handbook,* becoming a Peace Corps Volunteer entails certain safety risks. Living and traveling in an unfamiliar environment (oftentimes alone), having a limited understanding of local language and culture, and being perceived as well-off are some of the factors that can put a Volunteer at risk. Many Volunteers experience varying degrees of unwanted attention and harassment. Petty thefts and burglaries are not uncommon, and incidents of physical and sexual assault do occur, although most Tonga Volunteers complete their two years of service without incident. The Peace Corps has established procedures and policies designed to help you reduce your risks and enhance your safety and security. These procedures and policies, in addition to safety training, will be provided once you arrive in Tonga. Using these tools, you are expected to take responsibility for your safety and well-being.

Each staff member at the Peace Corps is committed to providing Volunteers with the support they need to successfully meet the challenges they will face to have a safe, healthy, and productive service. We encourage Volunteers and families to look at our safety and security information on the Peace Corps website at www.peacecorps.gov/safety.

Information on these pages gives messages on Volunteer health and Volunteer safety. There is a section titled —Safety and Security in Depth." Among topics addressed are the risks of serving as a Volunteer, posts' safety support systems, and emergency planning and communications.

Rewards and Frustrations

Although the potential for job satisfaction in Tonga is quite high, like all Volunteers, you will encounter frustrations. Because of limited resources, co-workers and community members may not always provide optimum support. In addition, the pace of work and life is slower than what most Americans are accustomed to, and some people you work with may be hesitant to accept new ways of thinking or doing things. For these reasons, the Peace Corps experience of adapting to a new culture and environment is often described as a series of emotional peaks and valleys.

You will be given a high degree of responsibility and independence in your work—perhaps more than in any other job you have had or will have. You will often find yourself in situations that require an ability to motivate yourself and your co-workers with little guidance from supervisors. It may be difficult to capture the tangible and intangible impact of your work immediately. Development is a slow process. Progress is often sustained only after the combined efforts of several Volunteers over the course of many years. You may also face periods of isolation.

While you are likely to be placed in a community or on an island within an hour's walk, bike ride, or boat ride from another Volunteer, there will be limited opportunities to gather with the majority of your fellow Volunteers. You must possess the self-confidence, patience, and vision to continue working toward long-term goals with remote peer support.

Another source of frustration to Peace Corps Volunteers is the use of corporal punishment in schools. Even though corporal punishment is forbidden in the Tonga education system, it still occurs in some schools. While some parents oppose this strongly, others consider it an effective way of discipline.

To overcome these difficulties and differences, you will need to exercise maturity, flexibility, open-mindedness, and resourcefulness. The Peace Corps staff, your co-workers, and fellow Volunteers will support you during times of challenge, as well as celebrate with you during moments of success. Judging by the experiences of former Volunteers, the peaks are well worth the difficult times, and most Volunteers leave Tonga feeling they have gained much more than they sacrificed during their service. If you are able to make the commitment to integrate into your community and work hard, you will be a successful Volunteer and develop meaningful, long-lasting friendships.

PEACE CORPS TRAINING

Pre-Service Training

Pre-service training (PST) is the first event within a competency-based training program that continues throughout your 27 months of service in Tonga. PST ensures that Volunteers are equipped with the knowledge, skills, and attitudes to effectively perform their jobs. On average, nine of 10 trainees are sworn in as Volunteers.

Pre-service training is conducted in Tonga and directed by the Peace Corps with participation from representatives of Tongan organizations, former Volunteers, and/or training contractors. The length of PST varies, usually ranging from 8-12 weeks, depending on the competencies required for the assignment. PC/Tonga measures achievement of learning and determines if trainees have successfully achieved competencies, including language standards, for swearing in as a Peace Corps Volunteer.

Throughout service, Volunteers strive to achieve performance competencies. Initially, PST affords the opportunity for trainees to develop and test their own resources. As a trainee, you will play an active role in self-education. You will be asked to decide how best to set and meet objectives and to find alternative solutions. You will be asked to prepare for an experience in which you will often have to take the initiative and accept responsibility for decisions. The success of your learning will be enhanced by your own effort to take responsibility for your learning and through sharing experiences with others.

Peace Corps training is founded on adult learning methods and often includes experiential —hands-on" applications such as conducting a participatory community needs assessment and facilitating groups. Successful training results in competence in various technical, linguistic, cross-cultural, health, and safety and security areas. Integrating into the community is usually one of the core competencies Volunteers strive to achieve both in PST and during the first several months of service. Successful sustainable development work is based on the local trust and confidence Volunteers build by living in, and respectfully integrating into, the Tongan community and culture. Trainees are prepared for this through a —homestay" experience, which often requires trainees to live with host families during PST. Integration into the community not only facilitates good working relationships, but it fosters language learning and cross-cultural acceptance and trust, which help ensure your health, safety, and security.

Woven into the competencies, the ability to communicate in the host country language is critical to being an effective Peace Corps Volunteer. So basic is this precept that it is spelled out in the Peace Corps Act: No person shall be assigned to duty as a Volunteer under this act in any foreign country or area unless at the time of such assignment he (or she) possesses such reasonable proficiency as his (or her) assignment requires in speaking the language of the country or area to which he (or she) is assigned.

Technical Training

Technical training will prepare you to work in Tonga by building on the skills you already have and helping you develop new skills in a manner appropriate to the needs of the country. The Peace Corps staff, Tonga experts, and current Volunteers will conduct the training program. Training places great emphasis on learning how to transfer the skills you have to the community in which you will serve as a Volunteer.

Technical training will include sessions on the general economic and political environment in Tonga and strategies for working within such a framework. You will review your technical sector's goals and will meet with the Tonga agencies and organizations that invited the Peace Corps to assist them. You will be supported and evaluated throughout the training to build the confidence and skills you need to undertake your project activities and be a productive member of your community.

Language Training

As a Peace Corps Volunteer, you will find that language skills are key to personal and professional satisfaction during your service. These skills are critical to your job performance, they help you integrate into your community, and they can ease your personal adaptation to the new surroundings. Therefore, language training is at the heart of the training program. You must successfully meet minimum language requirements to complete training and become a Volunteer. Tongan language instructors teach formal language classes five days a week in small groups of four to five people.

Your language training will incorporate a community-based approach. In addition to classroom time, you will be given assignments to work on outside of the classroom and with your host family. The goal is to get you to a point of basic social communication skills so you can practice and develop language skills further once you are at your site. Prior to being sworn in as a Volunteer, you will work on strategies to continue language studies during your service.

Cross-Cultural Training

As part of your pre-service training, you will live with a Tongan host family. This experience is designed to ease your transition to life at your site. Families go through an orientation conducted by Peace Corps staff to explain the purpose of pre-service training and to assist them in helping you adapt to living in Tonga. Many Volunteers form strong and lasting friendships with their host families.

Cross-cultural and community development training will help you improve your communication skills and understand your role as a facilitator of development. You will be exposed to topics such as community mobilization, conflict resolution, gender and development, nonformal and adult education strategies, and political structures.

Health Training

During pre-service training, you will be given basic medical training and information. You will be expected to practice preventive health care and to take responsibility for your own health by adhering to all medical policies. Trainees are required to attend all medical sessions. The topics include preventive health measures and minor and major medical issues that you might encounter while in Tonga. Nutrition, mental health, setting up a safe living compound, and how to avoid HIV/AIDS and other sexually transmitted diseases (STDs) are also covered.

Safety Training

During the safety training sessions, you will learn how to adopt a lifestyle that reduces your risks at home, at work, and during your travels. You will also learn appropriate, effective strategies for coping with unwanted attention and about your individual responsibility for promoting safety throughout your service.

Additional Trainings During Volunteer Service

In its commitment to institutionalize quality training, the Peace Corps has implemented a training system that provides Volunteers with continual opportunities to examine their commitment to Peace Corps service while increasing their technical and cross-cultural skills. During service, there are usually three training events. The titles and objectives for those trainings are as follows:

- In-service training: *Provides an opportunity for Volunteers to upgrade their technical, language, and project development skills while sharing their experiences and reaffirming their commitment after having served for three to six months.*

- Midterm conference (done in conjunction with technical sector in-service): *Assists Volunteers in reviewing their first year, reassessing their personal and project objectives, and planning for their second year of service.*

- Close-of-service conference: *Prepares Volunteers for the future after Peace Corps service and reviews their respective projects and personal experiences.*

The number, length, and design of these trainings are adapted to country-specific needs and conditions. The key to the training system is that training events are integrated and interrelated, from the pre-departure orientation through the end of your service, and are planned, implemented, and evaluated cooperatively by the training staff, Peace Corps staff, and Volunteers.

YOUR HEALTH CARE AND SAFETY IN TONGA

The Peace Corps' highest priority is maintaining the good health and safety of every Volunteer. Peace Corps medical programs emphasize the preventive, rather than the curative, approach to disease. The Peace Corps in Tonga maintains a clinic with a full-time medical officer, who takes care of Volunteers' primary health care needs. Additional medical services, such as testing and basic treatment, are also available in Tonga at local hospitals. If you become seriously ill, you will be transported either to an American-standard medical facility in the region or to the United States.

Health Issues in Tonga

Major health problems among Volunteers in Tonga are rare and are often the result of the Volunteer failing to take preventive measures to stay healthy. The most common health problems are minor ones that are also found in the United States, such as colds, diarrhea, sinus infections, headaches, dental problems, minor injuries, sexually transmitted diseases, emotional problems, and alcohol abuse. These problems may be more frequent or compounded by life in Tonga because certain environmental factors in the country raise the risk or exacerbate the severity of illnesses and injuries.

Malaria is not present in Tonga, nor is rabies, though there are many stray animals. Typhoid, dengue fever, measles, and tuberculosis are endemic in Tonga.

Helping You Stay Healthy

The Peace Corps will provide you with all the necessary inoculations, medications, and information to stay healthy. Upon your arrival in Tonga, you will receive a medical handbook. At the end of training, you will receive a medical kit with supplies to take care of mild illnesses and first aid needs. The contents of the kit are listed later in this chapter.

During pre-service training, you will have access to basic medical supplies through the medical officer. However, you will be responsible for your own supply of prescription drugs and any other specific medical supplies you require, as the Peace Corps will not order these items during training. Please bring a three-month supply of any prescription drugs you use, since they may not be available here and it may take several months for shipments to arrive.

You will have physicals at midservice and at the end of your service. If you develop a serious medical problem during your service, the medical officer in Tonga will consult with the Office of Medical Services in Washington, D.C. If it is determined that your condition cannot be treated in Tonga, you may be sent out of the country for further evaluation and care.

Maintaining Your Health

As a Volunteer, you must accept considerable responsibility for your own health. Proper precautions will significantly reduce your risk of serious illness or injury. The adage ―An ounce of prevention …" becomes extremely important in areas where diagnostic and treatment facilities are not up to the standards of the United States. The most important of your responsibilities in Tonga is to take preventive measures to stay healthy. Many illnesses that afflict Volunteers worldwide are entirely preventable if proper food and water precautions are taken. These illnesses include food poisoning, parasitic infections, hepatitis A, dysentery, Guinea worms, tapeworms, and typhoid fever. Your medical officer will discuss specific standards for water and food preparation in Tonga during pre-service training.

Abstinence is the only certain choice for preventing infection with HIV and other sexually transmitted diseases. You are taking risks if you choose to be sexually active. To lessen risk, use a condom every time you have sex. Whether your partner is a host country citizen, a fellow Volunteer, or anyone else, do not assume this person is free of HIV/AIDS or other STDs. You will receive more information from the medical officer about this important issue.

Volunteers are expected to adhere to an effective means of birth control to prevent an unplanned pregnancy. Your medical officer can help you decide on the most appropriate method to suit your individual needs. Contraceptive methods are available without charge from the medical officer.

It is critical to your health that you promptly report to the medical office or other designated facility for scheduled immunizations, and that you let the medical officer know immediately of significant illnesses and injuries.

Women's Health Information

Pregnancy is treated in the same manner as other Volunteer health conditions that require medical attention but also have programmatic ramifications. The Peace Corps is responsible for determining the medical risk and the availability of appropriate medical care if the Volunteer remains in-country. Given the circumstances under which Volunteers live and work in Peace Corps countries, it is rare that the Peace Corps' medical and programmatic standards for continued service during pregnancy can be met.

If feminine hygiene products are not available for you to purchase on the local market, the Peace Corps medical officer in Tonga will provide them. If you require a specific product, please bring a three-month supply with you.

Your Peace Corps Medical Kit

The Peace Corps medical officer will provide you with a kit that contains basic items necessary to prevent and treat illnesses that may occur during service. Kit items can be periodically restocked at the medical office.

Medical Kit Contents

Ace bandages

Adhesive tape

American Red Cross First Aid & Safety Handbook

Antacid tablets (Tums)

Antibiotic ointment (Bacitracin/Neomycin/Polymycin B)

Antiseptic antimicrobial skin cleaner (Hibiclens)

Band-Aids

Butterfly closures

Calamine lotion

Cepacol lozenges

Condoms

Dental floss

Diphenhydramine HCL 25 mg (Benadryl)

Insect repellent stick (Cutter's)

Iodine tablets (for water purification)

Lip balm (Chapstick)

Oral rehydration salts

Oral thermometer (Fahrenheit)

Pseudoephedrine HCL 30 mg (Sudafed)

Robitussin-DM lozenges (for cough)

Scissors

Sterile gauze pads

Tetrahydrozaline eyedrops (Visine)

Tinactin (antifungal cream)

Tweezers

Before You Leave: A Medical Checklist

If there has been any change in your health—physical, mental, or dental—since you submitted your examination reports to the Peace Corps, you must immediately notify the Office of Medical Services. Failure to disclose new illnesses, injuries, allergies, or pregnancy can endanger your health and may jeopardize your eligibility to serve.

If your dental exam was done more than a year ago, or if your physical exam is more than two years old, contact the Office of Medical Services to find out whether you need to update your records. If your dentist or Peace Corps dental consultant has recommended that you undergo dental treatment or repair, you must complete that work and make sure your dentist sends requested confirmation reports or X-rays to the Office of Medical Services.

If you wish to avoid having duplicate vaccinations, contact your physician's office to obtain a copy of your immunization record and bring it to your pre-departure orientation. If you have any immunizations prior to Peace Corps service, the Peace Corps cannot reimburse you for the cost. The Peace Corps will provide all the immunizations necessary for your overseas assignment, either at your pre-departure orientation or shortly after you arrive in Tonga. You do not need to begin taking malaria medication prior to departure.

Bring a three-month supply of any prescription or over-the-counter medication you use on a regular basis, including birth control pills. Although the Peace Corps cannot reimburse you for this three-month supply, it will order refills during your service. While awaiting shipment—which can take several months—you will be dependent on your own medication supply. The Peace Corps will not pay for herbal or nonprescribed medications, such as St. John's wort, glucosamine, selenium, or antioxidant supplements.

You are encouraged to bring copies of medical prescriptions signed by your physician. This is not a requirement, but they might come in handy if you are questioned in transit about carrying a three-month supply of prescription drugs.

If you wear eyeglasses, bring two pairs with you—a pair and a spare. If a pair breaks, the Peace Corps will replace them, using the information your doctor in the United States provided on the eyeglasses form during your examination. The Peace Corps discourages you from using contact lenses during your service to reduce your risk of developing a serious infection or other eye disease. Most Peace Corps countries do not have appropriate water and sanitation to support eye care with the use of contact lenses. The Peace Corps will not supply or replace contact lenses or associated solutions unless an ophthalmologist has recommended their use for a specific medical condition and the Peace Corps' Office of Medical Services has given approval.

If you are eligible for Medicare, are over 50 years of age, or have a health condition that may restrict your future participation in health care plans, you may wish to consult an insurance specialist about unique coverage needs before your departure. The Peace Corps will provide all necessary health care from the time you leave for your pre-departure orientation until you complete your service. When you finish, you will be entitled to the post-service health care benefits described in the Peace Corps *Volunteer Handbook*. You may wish to consider keeping an existing health plan in effect during your service if you think age or pre-existing conditions might prevent you from re-enrolling in your current plan when you return home.

Safety and Security—Our Partnership

Serving as a Volunteer overseas entails certain safety and security risks. Living and traveling in an unfamiliar environment, a limited understanding of the local language and culture, and the perception of being a wealthy American are some of the factors that can put a Volunteer at risk. Property theft and burglaries are not uncommon. Incidents of physical and sexual assault do occur, although almost all Volunteers complete their two years of service without serious personal safety problems.

Beyond knowing that Peace Corps approaches safety and security as a partnership with you, it might be helpful to see how this partnership works. Peace Corps has policies, procedures, and training in place to promote your safety. We depend on you to follow those policies and to put into practice what you have learned. An example of how this works in practice—in this case to help manage the risk of burglary—is:

- Peace Corps assesses the security environment where you will live and work
- Peace Corps inspects the house where you will live according to established security criteria
- Peace Corps provides you with resources to take measures such as installing new locks
- Peace Corps ensures you are welcomed by host country authorities in your new community
- Peace Corps responds to security concerns that you raise
- You lock your doors and windows
- You adopt a lifestyle appropriate to the community where you live
- You get to know neighbors
- You decide if purchasing personal articles insurance is appropriate for you
- You don't change residences before being authorized by Peace Corps
- You communicate concerns that you have to Peace Corps staff

This *Welcome Book* contains sections on: Living Conditions and Volunteer Lifestyle; Peace Corps Training; and Your Health Care and Safety that all include important safety and security information to help you understand this partnership. The Peace Corps makes every effort to give Volunteers the tools they need to function in the safest way possible, because working to maximize the safety and security of Volunteers is our highest priority. Not only do we provide you with training and tools to prepare for the unexpected, but we teach you to identify, reduce, and manage the risks you may encounter.

Factors that Contribute to Volunteer Risk

There are several factors that can heighten a Volunteer's risk, many of which are within the Volunteer's control. By far the most common crime that Volunteers experience are thefts. Thefts often occur when Volunteers are away from their sites, in crowded locations (such as markets or on public transportation), and when leaving items unattended. House break-ins, theft, and burglary are the most prevelant crimes against Volunteers in Tonga, as you can see from the graphs below.

Before you depart for Tonga there are several measures you can take to reduce your risk:

- Leave valuable objects in the U.S.
- Leave copies of important documents and account numbers in the U.S. with someone you trust.
- Purchase a hidden money pouch or "dummy" wallet as a decoy
- Purchase personal articles insurance

After you arrive in Tonga, you will receive more detailed information about common crimes, factors that contribute to Volunteer risk, and local strategies to reduce that risk. For example, Volunteers in Tonga learn to:

- Choose safe routes and times for travel, and travel with someone trusted by the community whenever possible

- Make sure one's personal appearance is respectful of local customs

- Avoid high-crime areas

- Know the local language to get help in an emergency

- Make friends with local people who are respected in the community

- Limit alcohol consumption

As you can see from this list, you must be willing to work hard and adapt your lifestyle to minimize the potential for being a target for crime. As with anywhere in the world, crime does exist in Tonga. You can reduce your risk by avoiding situations that place you at risk and by taking precautions. Crime at the village or town level is less frequent than in the large cities; people know each other and generally are less likely to steal from their neighbors. Tourist attractions in large towns are favorite worksites for pickpockets.

The following are other security concerns in Tonga of which you should be aware:

Being in an island environment, lots of people travel by small boats. Water safety and transportation can be dangerous and will affect your safety if you become complacent. During your time in Tonga you will be instructed on how to live around the water while still being confident in and respectful of it.

Being a foreigner, you may be subject to harrassment which may be benign or serious. Learning to speak the local language, integration into your community, and cultural sensitivity are all keys to diffusing harrassment and will allow you to escape threats to your personal safety. Remember, sexual harrassment is not a crime in Tonga.

Staying Safe: Don't Be a Target for Crime

You must be prepared to take on a large degree of responsibility for your own safety. You can make yourself less of a target, ensure that your home is secure, and develop relationships in your community that will make you an unlikely victim of crime. While the factors that contribute to your risk in Tonga may be different, in many ways you can do what you would do if you moved to a new city anywhere: Be cautious, check things out, ask questions, learn about your neighborhood, know where the more risky locations are, use common sense, and be aware. You can reduce your vulnerability to crime by integrating into your community, learning the local language, acting responsibly, and abiding by Peace Corps policies and procedures. Serving safely and effectively in Tonga will require that you accept some restrictions on your current lifestyle.

Support from Staff

If a trainee or Volunteer is the victim of a safety incident, Peace Corps staff is prepared to provide support. All Peace Corps posts have procedures in place to respond to incidents of crime committed against Volunteers. The first priority for all posts in the aftermath of an incident is to ensure the Volunteer is safe and receiving medical treatment as needed. After assuring the safety of the Volunteer, Peace Corps staff response may include reassessing the Volunteer's worksite and housing arrangements and making any adjustments, as needed. In some cases, the nature of the incident may necessitate a site or housing transfer. Peace Corps staff will also assist Volunteers with preserving their rights to pursue legal sanctions against the perpetrators of the crime. It is very important that Volunteers report incidents as they occur, not only to protect their peer Volunteers, but also to preserve the future right to prosecute. Should Volunteers decide later in the process that they want to proceed with the prosecution of their assailant, this option may no longer exist if the evidence of the event has not been preserved at the time of the incident.

Crime Data for Tonga

Crime data and statistics for Tonga, which is updated yearly, are available at the following link:

http://www.peacecorps.gov/countrydata/tonga

Please take the time to review this important information.

Few Peace Corps Volunteers are victims of serious crimes and crimes that do occur overseas are investigated and prosecuted by local authorities through the local courts system. If you are the victim of a crime, you will decide if you wish to pursue prosecution. If you decide to prosecute, Peace Corps will be there to assist you. One of our tasks is to ensure you are fully informed of your options and understand how the local legal process works. Peace Corps will help you ensure your rights are protected to the fullest extent possible under the laws of the country.

If you are the victim of a serious crime, you will learn how to get to a safe location as quickly as possible and contact your Peace Corps office. It's important that you notify Peace Corps as soon as you can so Peace Corps can provide you with the help you need.

Volunteer Safety Support in Tonga

The Peace Corps' approach to safety is a five-pronged plan to help you stay safe during your service and includes the following: information sharing, Volunteer training, site selection criteria, a detailed emergency action plan, and protocols for addressing safety and security incidents. Tonga's in-country safety program is outlined below.

The Peace Corps/Tonga office will keep you informed of any issues that may impact Volunteer safety through **information sharing**. Regular updates will be provided in Volunteer newsletters and in memorandums from the country director. A weekly email is sent to all volunteers with latest crime updates, weather forecasts and any other information relevent to your safety. In the event of a critical situation or emergency, you will be contacted through the emergency communication network. An important component of the capacity of Peace Corps to keep you informed is your buy-in to the partnership concept with the Peace Corps staff. It is expected that you will do your part in ensuring that Peace Corps staff members are kept apprised of your movements in-country so they are able to inform you.

Volunteer training will include sessions on specific safety and security issues in Tonga. This training will prepare you to adopt a culturally appropriate lifestyle and exercise judgment that promotes safety and reduces risk in your home, at work, and while traveling. Safety training is offered throughout service and is integrated into the language, cross-cultural aspects, health, and other components of training. You will be expected to successfully complete all training competencies in a variety of areas, including safety and security, as a condition of service.

Certain **site selection criteria** are used to determine safe housing for Volunteers before their arrival. The Peace Corps staff works closely with host communities and counterpart agencies to help prepare them for a Volunteer's arrival and to establish expectations of their respective roles in supporting the Volunteer. Each site is inspected before the Volunteer's arrival to ensure placement in appropriate, safe, and secure housing and worksites.

Site selection is based, in part, on any relevant site history; access to medical, banking, postal, and other essential services; availability of communications, transportation, and markets; different housing options and living arrangements; and other Volunteer support needs.

You will be given a copy of PC/Tonga's Emergency Action Plan, which outlines strategies related to emergencies involving natural disasters such as cyclones, earthquakes, tsunamis, and civil unrest. It contains explicit explanations of each event and has detailed the roles and responsibilities of Volunteers during any type of emergency.

When you arrive at your site, you will complete and submit a site locator form with your address, contact information, and a map to your house. If there is a security threat, you will gather with other Volunteers in Tonga at predetermined locations until the situation is resolved or the Peace Corps decides to evacuate.

Finally, in order for the Peace Corps to be fully responsive to the needs of Volunteers, it is imperative that Volunteers immediately report any security incident to the Peace Corps office. The Peace Corps has established **protocols for addressing safety and security incidents** in a timely and appropriate manner, and it collects and evaluates safety and security data to track trends and develop strategies to minimize risks to future Volunteers.

DIVERSITY AND CROSS-CULTURAL ISSUES

In fulfilling its mandate to share the face of America with host countries, the Peace Corps is making special efforts to assure that all of America's richness is reflected in the Volunteer corps. More Americans of color are serving in today's Peace Corps than at any time in recent history. Differences in race, ethnic background, age, religion, and sexual orientation are expected and welcomed among our Volunteers. Part of the Peace Corps' mission is to help dispel any notion that Americans are all of one origin or race and to establish that each of us is as thoroughly American as the other despite our many differences.

Our diversity helps us accomplish that goal. In other ways, however, it poses challenges. In Tonga, as in other Peace Corps host countries, Volunteers' behavior, lifestyle, background, and beliefs are judged in a cultural context very different from their own. Certain personal perspectives or characteristics commonly accepted in the United States may be quite uncommon, unacceptable, or even repressed in Tonga.

Outside of Tonga's capital, residents of rural communities have had relatively little direct exposure to other cultures, races, religions, and lifestyles. What people view as typical American behavior or norms may be a misconception, such as the belief that all Americans are rich and have blond hair and blue eyes. The people of Tonga are justly known for their generous hospitality to foreigners; however, members of the community in which you will live may display a range of reactions to cultural differences that you present.

To ease the transition and adapt to life in Tonga, you may need to make some temporary, yet fundamental compromises in how you present yourself as an American and as an individual. For example, female trainees and Volunteers may not be able to exercise the independence available to them in the United States; political discussions need to be handled with great care; and some of your personal beliefs may best remain undisclosed. You will need to develop techniques and personal strategies for coping with these and other limitations.

The Peace Corps staff will lead diversity and sensitivity discussions during pre-service training and will be on call to provide support, but the challenge ultimately will be your own.

Overview of Diversity in Tonga

The Peace Corps staff in Tonga recognizes the adjustment issues that come with diversity and will endeavor to provide support and guidance. During pre-service training, several sessions will be held to discuss diversity and coping mechanisms. We look forward to having male and female Volunteers from a variety of races, ethnic groups, ages, religions, and sexual orientations, and hope that you will become part of a diverse group of Americans who take pride in supporting one another and demonstrating the richness of American culture.

What Might a Volunteer Face?

Possible Issues for Female Volunteers

Tonga has a traditional, patriarchal culture. Although women have achieved high rank in government ministries, people at the community level have not had much experience with women who take on professional roles or who live independently of their families. Most women in Tonga do very little independently and generally travel, even if it is just to the corner shop to buy flour, with at least one other person. This does not mean female Volunteers cannot live or do things on their own, but they need to be aware that the community in which they live may view their behavior as strange.

Many Tongans have large, robust figures, which are considered desirable in traditional Tongan culture, although perceptions are changing. Slender women may be told they are too skinny, while larger women may be told they are fat in what is intended as a compliment.

Female Volunteers in Tonga often receive an inordinate amount of attention from Tongan men. Flirting, ogling, catcalls, and a certain amount of protective behavior by host family and community members are common. Females are often asked about their marital status and whether they would like to marry someone locally. Most of the attention is good-natured and can be fended off with humorous replies.

Because Tongans do not engage in friendships with members of the opposite sex, it is culturally inappropriate for a female Volunteer to entertain a man (or men) alone in her home, whether the man is Tongan or another Volunteer. Her community is likely to view such a situation as a romantic or sexual relationship. Female Volunteers in Tonga have occasionally had people peep in their windows or appear in their homes without invitation or warning.

Possible Issues for Volunteers of Color

Some African-American and Asian-American Volunteers have been annoyed or frustrated when Tongans tell them they —look just like we do." An Asian American may be called *mata'i Siapani* (—Japanese eyes") or *mata'i Siaina* (—Chinese eyes"). African-American Volunteers are sometimes referred to by Tongans as —Nka," but without the offensive connotation associated with the similar American slur. However, when Volunteers become known to their communities, being of color has not negatively impacted their ability to serve effectively.

Some Asian Americans may hear "*Siaina*" or "*Siapani*" mixed with some mock Chinese words called out to them from across the street or whispered to a friend two feet away. The name calling can be ignored, but it may represent ignorance of, or discomfort with, diversity. Most Tongans cannot distinguish between the Chinese immigrants and Asians from other countries, so all Asians, including Asian Americans, tend to be grouped with the Chinese immigrants. This makes Asian-American Volunteers potential targets for ethnically motivated crimes. Bars that might be acceptable for other Volunteers might be unsafe for you. Above all else, use common sense.

That said, ethnic prejudice against Asians in Tonga is complex. A number of Chinese immigrants have worked hard to adopt the Tongan language and to integrate effectively. During the Nuku'alofa riot on November 16, 2006, some Chinese immigrants were protected by Tongan friends and neighbors. Also, as much as some Tongans complain about Chinese stores and business practices, these stores are increasingly popular and arguably essential to the economic well-being of the Kingdom.

To be an effective Asian-American Volunteer, it is necessary to integrate into the community. Let people know what a Peace Corps Volunteer is, that you come from America, and what your Volunteer work is. Adopting the native Tongan attire will also immediately identify you as someone who is trying to learn about and respect the Tongan way of life.

Possible Issues for Senior Volunteers

Respect and courtesy are extended to both male and female seniors in Tonga, and senior Volunteers are likely to be given places of high honor. Out of respect for their age, Tongans often discourage senior Volunteers from physical activity and exertion. Senior Volunteers may also find that they are one of the few Volunteers, if not the only Volunteer, of their age in their training group.

Possible Issues for Gay, Lesbian, or Bisexual Volunteers

Tongan sexual mores are fairly strict, and unmarried males and females are relatively separated. Male homosexual relationships are very discreet, though not totally uncommon. In Tonga, there is a concept called *fakaleiti,* whereby boys are raised as girls and take on the appearance and social responsibilities of women. This is often done in households that do not have a female child to help with chores around the house. *Fakaleitis* in Tonga may or may not be associated with homosexuality, though homosexuals are definitely associated with fakaleiti. Male Volunteers who engage in typically female dominated chores in Tonga are often met with laughter and called *fakaleiti.* Such laughing and joking tends to be very harmless, as *fakaleitis* have long been an accepted part of the Tongan culture. You will learn more about this cultural phenomenon during pre-service training.

Homosexual relationships in Tonga are not well researched and documented, but the frequency and explicitness of homosexual jokes and references suggests a prevalence that has not been openly acknowledged. Though not necessarily connected, many Volunteers observe Tongan males to be comfortable with holding another man's hand or walking down the street with their arms around another man's shoulder.

Lesbianism in Tonga is nearly invisble (people may say it is nonexistant), and discussions of it are often responded to with derision or disbelief. This can pose unique challenges for gay women serving in Tonga, especially related to effectively coping with the cultural norms around sexuality.

While cross-dressing for men is acceptable, there are laws against homosexual practices, so having a gay partner of either sex can cause issues with friends, colleagues, and even possibly the law. It is best to be extremely discreet about this until well into your service, when you can better assess the mood of the community.

A recommended resource for support and advice prior to and during your service is the Lesbian, Gay, Bisexual & Transgender U.S. Peace Corps Alumni website at www.lgbrpcv.org.

Possible Religious Issues for Volunteers

The overwhelming majority of Tongans are Christian, and attending church and observing holy days are important activities in every community. On Sundays, for example, recreation is forbidden by law. Regardless of their own faith, many Volunteers choose to attend church to show respect for local customs and to develop relationships in their communities. The Peace Corps encourages Volunteers of every religious/spiritual persuasion to recognize the church as an important community institution and to participate accordingly.

Volunteers who are worried about the religious/spiritual nature of this participation can consult with their peers or Volunteers from previous groups on how to tactfully work in a church-dominant society while maintaining one's own religious/spiritual beliefs. Many Volunteers who have been particularly concerned about this aspect of serving in Tonga have observed that attending services is a way of showing respect for local customs and helps develop relationships in the communities.

Possible Issues for Volunteers With Disabilities

As part of the medical clearance process, the Peace Corps Office of Medical Services determined that you were physically and emotionally capable, with or without reasonable accommodations, to perform a full tour of Volunteer service in-country without unreasonable risk of harm to yourself or interruption of service.

Tongans generally treat people with disabilities with respect. The main challenge will be that the accommodations you are accustomed to having in the United States may not be available locally. Nevertheless, the Peace Corps/Tonga staff will work with you to make reasonable accommodations in training, housing, and jobsites to enable you to serve safely and effectively.

FREQUENTLY ASKED QUESTIONS

This list has been compiled by Volunteers serving in Tonga and is based on their experience. Use it as an informal guide in making your own list, bearing in mind that each experience is individual. There is no perfect list! You obviously cannot bring everything on the list, so consider those items that make the most sense to you personally and professionally. You can always have things sent to you later. As you decide what to bring, keep in mind that you have a 100-pound weight limit on baggage. And remember, you can get almost everything you need in Tonga.

How much luggage am I allowed to bring to Tonga?

Most airlines have baggage size and weight limits and assess charges for transport of baggage that exceeds those limits. The Peace Corps has its own size and weight limits and will not pay the cost of transport for baggage that exceeds these limits. The Peace Corps' allowance is two checked pieces of luggage with combined dimensions of both pieces not to exceed 107 inches (length + width + height) and a carry-on bag with dimensions of no more than 45 inches. Checked baggage should not exceed 100 pounds total with a maximum weight of 50 pounds for any one bag.

Peace Corps Volunteers are not allowed to take pets, weapons, explosives, radio transmitters (shortwave radios are permitted), automobiles, or motorcycles to their overseas assignments. Do not pack flammable materials or liquids such as lighter fluid, cleaning solvents, hair spray, or aerosol containers. This is an important safety precaution.

What is the electric current in Tonga?

The current in Tonga is 220 volts, 50 cycles, with variations. The variations can be extreme at times, so be prepared to take protective measures for any electronic equipment you bring. Many Volunteers in Tonga have electricity in their homes at least some of the time, including that produced by solar power or gas generators. Most Volunteers placed on the outer islands have electricity between specific evening and nighttime hours while a few have no electricity

How much money should I bring?

Volunteers are expected to live at the same level as the people in their community. You will be given a settling-in allowance and a monthly living allowance, which should cover your expenses. Volunteers often wish to bring additional money for vacation travel to other countries. Credit cards and traveler's checks are preferable to cash. If you choose to bring extra money, bring the amount that will suit your own travel plans and needs.

When can I take vacation and have people visit me?

Each Volunteer accrues two vacation days per month of service (excluding training). Leave may not be taken during training, the first three months of service, or the last two months of service, except in conjunction with an authorized emergency leave. Family and friends are welcome to visit you after pre-service training and the first three months of service as long as their stay does not interfere with your work. Extended stays at your site (more than two weeks) are not encouraged and require permission from your country director. The Peace Corps is not able to provide your visitors with visa, medical, or travel assistance.

Will my belongings be covered by insurance?

The Peace Corps does not provide insurance coverage for personal effects; Volunteers are ultimately responsible for the safekeeping of their personal belongings. However, you can purchase personal property insurance before you leave. If you wish, you may contact your own insurance company; additionally, insurance application forms will be provided, and we encourage you to consider them carefully. Volunteers should not ship or take valuable items overseas. Jewelry, watches, radios, cameras, and expensive appliances are subject to loss, theft, and breakage, and in many places, satisfactory maintenance and repair services are not available.

Do I need an international driver's license?

Volunteers in Tonga do not need an international driver's license because they are prohibited from operating privately owned motorized vehicles. Most urban travel is by bus or taxi. Rural travel ranges from buses and minibuses to trucks, bicycles, and lots of walking. On very rare occasions, a Volunteer may be asked to drive a sponsor's vehicle, but this can occur only with prior written permission from the country director. Should this occur, the Volunteer may obtain a local driver's license. A U.S. driver's license will facilitate the process, so bring it with you just in case. (You may also want to use it for renting a car when on leave in a non-Peace Corps country.)

What should I bring as gifts for Tongan friends and my host family?

This is not a requirement. A token of friendship is sufficient. Some gift suggestions include knickknacks for the house; pictures, books, or calendars of American scenes; souvenirs from your area; hard candies that will not melt or spoil; or photos to give away.It is a really good idea to bring pictures of your family and community to show Tongas where and how you live.

Where will my site assignment be when I finish training and how isolated will I be?

Peace Corps trainees are not assigned to individual sites until after they have completed pre-service training. This gives Peace Corps staff the opportunity to assess each trainee's technical and language skills prior to assigning sites, in addition to finalizing site selections with their ministry counterparts. If feasible, you may have the opportunity to provide input on your site preferences, including geographical location, distance from other Volunteers, and living conditions. However, keep in mind that many factors influence the site selection process and that the Peace Corps cannot guarantee placement where you would ideally like to be. Most Volunteers live in small towns or in rural villages and are usually within one hour from another Volunteer.

How can my family contact me in an emergency?

The Peace Corps' Counseling and Outreach Unit provides assistance in handling emergencies affecting trainees and Volunteers or their families. Before leaving the United States, instruct your family to notify the Counseling and Outreach Unit immediately if an emergency arises, such as a serious illness or death of a family member. During normal business hours, the number for the Counseling and Outreach Unit is 800.424.8580; select option 2, then extension 1470. After normal business hours and on weekends and holidays, the Counseling and Outreach Unit duty officer can be reached at the above number. For non-emergency questions, your family can get information from your country desk staff at the Peace Corps by calling 800.424.8580.

Can I call home from Tonga?

Yes, it is possible to purchase a local telephone card to call the United States. Some Volunteers use Skype for their communication with family and friends back home.

Should I bring a cellular phone with me?

Tonga has two mobile phone systems. The only mobile phones compatible with the systems here are tri-band phones, which utilize SIM cards. Most mobile phones from the U.S. are not compatible and Volunteers find it easiest to purchase mobile phones in Tonga. If you do bring a phone from home, you will have to pay a fee to have it "unlocked" from the U.S. system before it can work in Tonga.

Will there be email and Internet access?
Should I bring my computer?

There is email and Internet access at businesses in the capital; at the Peace Corps offices on the main island, _Eua, and Vava'u; and possibly through your host organization. Because of weaker telephone and electrical infrastructure in outlying areas, Volunteers in rural sites may be limited to sending and receiving email on their occasional visits to the capital or city center of their island group. Some Volunteers have brought laptop computers, but they are responsible for insuring and maintaining these computers.

Be aware that you will probably not find the same level of technical assistance and service in Tonga as you would at home and that replacement parts could take months to arrive. (See the earlier Living Conditions and Volunteer Lifestyle section for more information).

WELCOME LETTERS FROM TONGA VOLUNTEERS

Dear Future Volunteers,

Mālō e lelei! Congratulations on arriving at this step of the application process and receiving an invitation to serve in the Kingdom of Tonga! If you have already found Tonga on the map, (which was the first thing I had to do!) you are probably excited about spending your years of Peace Corps service in an island paradise.

Of course there is much more to Tonga than palm trees and coconuts. Throughout your service, you will have the opportunity to work alongside men, women, youth, and children who are part of a vibrant and unique culture. You will learn to speak Tongan, wear a *ta'ovala*, cook food wrapped in taro leaves in an underground oven, and maybe even learn to dance a *tau'olunga* or *ma'ulu'ulu*.

As a TEFL Volunteer, you will be placed in a primary school in a rural village. While I was teaching, my students became my inspiration and energy. They were enthusiastic about learning and loved using English. I could always count on them to lovingly tease me about my mistakes in Tongan and to teach me as much, or even more, than I could ever teach them.

Members of your village may even become like family when they invite you to church and feed you a delicious Sunday meal of *lū, 'ufi,* and *kumala*. While they may constantly ask you to help them or their families with English and to write letters, they will always offer something in return.

Community is such an important aspect of the Tongan culture, and as Peace Corps Volunteers, we have the amazing opportunity to become part of it. I spent the first two years of my service in a small rural village on the main island of Tongatapu. The teachers, principal, parents, and students worked hard to ensure that I was not *ta'elata* (homesick). They brought me more food than I could eat and sent their kids over to make sure I was never lonely. I had to learn to take bike rides or to sneak off with a book in order to find my own time!

Of course there are and always will be ups and downs. But one of the best parts of Peace Corps is the opportunity to learn more about this country, the people, and especially yourself. For most Volunteers, the ups clearly overshadow the downs. I especially found that to be true and I have even extended my service for a third year. I now work in the capital, Nuku'alofa, for the Ministry of Education and for the Peace Corps office as one of the Volunteer leaders. I am using the experiences from my village in a new and challenging way.

Finally, as you prepare for your journey, I would like to offer a few ideas for you. The overused phrases of ―flexibility" and an "open mind" are overused for a reason. And in Tonga, a ―sense of humor" and the ability to laugh at yourself will help you through the inevitable culture shock as you form lifelong friendships.

So pack those three things, a bottle of sunscreen, and something fun, and you will be at the beginning two (or three if you are like me!) years. Good luck, safe travels, and we'll see you in Tonga!

'Ofa atu,

Meredith Clarkson

Peace Corps Volunteer Leader (2009-2013)

Dear Future Volunteers:

Malo e lelei and congratulations on your placement in the Kingdom of Tonga! You're about to embark on an exciting journey that will not only lend you a chance to help this wonderful country, but will provide the unique opportunity to learn more about the culture, the beliefs, and the traditions of the people of the Friendly Islands.

Are you prepared to learn how to properly pronounce a glottal stop, how to dance the *tau'olunga* or *mako*, how to properly wear a *ta'ovala*, how to fish with a spear, how to cook your catch underground, and how to eat it with your hands? Most importantly, are you ready to laugh at yourself while doing all of that? If all that sounds a bit overwhelming, don't worry. Your first 2½ months will be spent in a rigorous training session with a focus on language and technical training. During this time, you'll stay with a host family who will help to gently guide you through the cultural and linguistic labyrinth. You'll also get to know your fellow trainees and see some of the beautiful sights Tonga has to offer. Before the end of this training, you'll be prepared for working at your site, well-versed in Tongan traditions and beliefs, and telling jokes about it all … in Tongan.

After swearing in, you'll head to your site. Now, when most people think of life in the Peace Corps, they imagine slowing down, sleeping in austere grass huts without modern conveniences like electricity and running water, cooking outdoors, communicating with family back home via old-fashioned letters, and speaking only the local language. While some of these visions come true for some Volunteers here in Tonga, other visions of Peace Corps life here may surprise you. Most Volunteers have electricity, cellphones, attend weekly Christian church services, and speak at least a little English in their workplaces. Some have Internet and washing machines in their houses, while others rely on kerosene lamps and satellite phones. Volunteers' working conditions also vary greatly. Secondary projects offer a chance to expand into other areas of service. Volunteers run libraries or computer labs, hold cooking or exercise classes, find ways to dispose of electronic or toxic waste, find funding for community needs like water tanks, write blogs to help Americans better understand Tongans, and help plan a weeklong girls' empowerment camp. The possibilities are endless!

Your experience will depend not only on your site, but also on you. The Peace Corps is really what you make of it. You've likely heard this already, but it bears repeating: you get what you put into your service. So eat your favorite foods, hug your family and friends, throw at least one fun thing into your suitcase, and set your watch to ―Tonga Time." Your adventure is only beginning!

Jennifer Bohn

Peace Corps Volunteer (2009-2011)

Dear Future Volunteers,

Malo e lelei and welcome to Peace Corps/Tonga! Congratulations on completing the marathon that is the Peace Corps application process. I can remember the summer before I came to Tonga; I checked my email daily to see if there were updates on my application status. It was an exciting time and I had so many questions: Will I have running water? Will I have electricity? What will my Peace Corps experience be like? I read many different blogs and couldn't wait to get here and start my adventure. All of the blogs mention to come without preconceived expectations, and let me tell you, your Peace Corps service will be the adventure of a lifetime and nothing at all like what you expected.

Everyone's Peace Corps experience is going to be different but here is a glimpse into my life in an outer village of Vava'u. During my first year, I focused primarily on teaching and organizing the school library. My secondary projects centered mostly around my school: I started a banana circle to compost organic waste, planted a school vegetable garden to raise money for the PTA, and received funding to give the library upgraded bookshelves and a paint job. My teaching experience in America proved beneficial in the Tongan classroom, but that didn't mean I wasn't nervous teaching to non-English speakers. However, once I was in front of the class, I found myself acting out instructions to properly convey my messages and the students enjoyed the animation. I soon realized a key to exciting lessons and classroom management is competition. Tongan students of all ages respond well to competition. It encourages teamwork, forces students to discipline themselves, and creates a fun and interactive environment in which to learn. Teaching will be both rewarding and challenging, and like your Peace Corps experience, some things will work out and some won't, but at the end of the day something always makes you smile.

In my second year, after becoming more comfortable with the community's needs and wants, I started focusing on projects outside of school. I helped organize a women's group in the village, led strategic planning workshops, and helping them determine their vision and goals. We researched different grants and eventually secured funding for the group to buy materials to begin their own organic garden. I also worked with my town officer to find funding for community toilets at different places throughout the village. These projects have been successful because of my relationships within the community. The community sought out my help, and the projects were their own creation. The community was able to take ownership of the projects and see their goals come to fruition.

I hope this letter has given you an idea of some things you can do in your new home. Try not to be overwhelmed and let things come to you naturally, make yourself available, stay flexible, and the work will come. And don't forget to really experience it all! While 27 months may seem like a long time now, it will fly by, so soak it up and allow the Peace Corps experience to take over. The Peace Corps will positively impact you in ways you cannot yet imagine, and while there will be both ups and downs, the ups will far outweigh the downs. It will be hard to be so far from things familiar, away from family and friends, but the group you come here with will quickly become your new family, and you will make lifelong friendships with people from all walks of life. Good luck and enjoy the adventure, wherever it takes you.

Sincerely,

Brandon Beebe

Peace Corps Volunteer (2010-2012)

PACKING LIST

This list has been compiled by Volunteers serving in Tonga and is based on their experience. Use it as an informal guide in making your own list, bearing in mind that each experience is individual. There is no perfect list! You obviously cannot bring everything on the list, so consider those items that make the most sense to you personally and professionally. You can always have things sent to you later. As you decide what to bring, keep in mind that you have a 100-pound weight limit on baggage. And remember, you can get almost everything you need in Tonga.

General Clothing

Hand washing and Tongan weather are hard on clothing, so any clothing you bring will probably wear out. Lightweight, fast-drying clothing (polyester or nylon) is nice because it will not fade or stretch as much as cotton blends.

Dressing in a culturally appropriate manner is important, especially on outer islands. In professional settings, male Volunteers are expected to wear what Tongan men wear—a *tupenu*, a solid-color wraparound garment (purchased locally), with a button-down shirt. During leisure time, Tongan men typically wear the same things men wear in the United States (e.g., below-the-knee shorts or slacks and T-shirts). Female Volunteers are expected to wear dresses or skirts that are midcalf or longer in both professional settings and during leisure time. If the dresses/skirts are not long enough, long wraparound underskirts are available locally. Excessively tight clothing is also culturally inappropriate. At home, women often wear loose-fitting slacks, capris pants, or below-the-knee shorts. In general, women should always cover their shoulders and knees and should not wear shorts except for swimming or exercising. Additionally, you should not be able to see your armpits or midriff when raising your arms.

Following are some specific clothing suggestions and recommendations:

- One sweatshirt or fleece (it can get a bit chilly in the winter)

- Lightweight rain jacket

- Black clothing to wear to funerals or to show mourning

- Swimsuit or board shorts for vacations (women will only be able to wear a swimsuit in Tonga at resorts)

- Underwear (with sturdy elastic) and socks for exercise

- High-quality flip-flops (e.g., Tevas, Chacos, or Reef walkers), nice sandals for special events, sneakers, hiking boots, and shoes for staging

For Men

- Six to eight light T-shirts

- Jeans and lightweight pants (khakis or linen) (you will be wearing a traditional tupenu every day to work and church)

- Several lightweight, collared, short-sleeved, button-down shirts and nice polos (enough for work and church, for every day but Saturday) and at least one tie and a long-sleeved shirt to go with it

- Basketball shorts for your own house or exercise

- Shorts that go to at least your knee for going out on evenings and weekends

<u>For Women</u>

Note: all dresses and skirts should be at midcalf or ankle length and blouses should not be sleeveless, see-through, or have bare midriffs!

- At least three black outfits: either a dress with sleeves or a skirt and top

- Casual dresses or mix-and-match skirts and blouses (for work, walking in public, and church)

- Underwear, bras, and sports bras (wick-away fabric [e.g., Coolmax] is effective)

- Undershirts or camisoles for sheer blouses

- One or two pairs of capris or lightweight long pants; bring jeans for colder weather

- Bike shorts for modesty and comfort under skirts (remember that Tonga is very humid)

- Board shorts for swimming in public places

Personal Hygiene and Toiletry Items
- Towels (lightweight ones are preferable to thick ones due to hand washing and drying time); also a travel towel (micro-fiber)

- Initial supply of your favorite shampoo, deodorant, perfume, etc. (Offensive odors are particularly objectionable in Tongan culture); deodorant is available in Tonga, but the quality is poor

- Cosmetics, if you wear them (local products generally are not of good quality)

- Six-month supply of tampons or pads (tampons are not always available in Tonga, and they are expensive)

- Hand sanitizer (e.g., Purell) and liquid body wash

- Vitamins, preferred medications (like, Excedrin), or dietary supplements

- Baby powder or talcum powder

- Small mirror

- Contact solution supply for six months if you wear contacts–it's not available everywhere in Tonga and is very expensive

- Razors–bring a few to start with, you can get cheaper quality ones here

Kitchen
(Many of these items can be found in Tonga, but are of reduced quality.)

- Swiss army knife, Leatherman, or other utility tool

- Sharp kitchen knife

- Nonstick frying pan

- Sturdy manual can opener

- A French press or stove-top espresso maker (if you like coffee); instant coffee is available here, but decaf coffee is not

- Measuring spoons and cups

- Spices/hot sauce (e.g., Tabasco)

- Vegetable holder (three-basket, hanging)

Miscellaneous

Luggage: lockable rolling duffel bags work best. Please keep in mind that you should be able to manage all of your luggage without the assistance of others. You may also want a smaller bag to use for your pre-service training homestay.

- Small backpack or shoulder bag

- Sheets (double flats are most useful)

- Sturdy water bottles (at least two; e.g., Nalgene or camel back)

- Camera: 35 mm or digital is recommended. Also consider an underwater camera. Film processing and printing is expensive and only available on Tongatapu and Vava'u. Consider extra memory cards and batteries

- Flashlight or headlamp (LED preferred) and/or reading lamp/book light

- Mask and snorkel or swimming goggles

- Small sewing kit

- Rain jacket

- Rechargeable batteries and charger (batteries are available, but are generally of poor quality and there is no way to properly dispose of them)

- MP3 player (e.g., iPod) or small "boombox" and small speakers

- Bicycle (some Volunteers highly recommend bringing one because of the poor quality of local brands; others say bringing one is not worth the added weight). If you decide to bring a bicycle, then a bicycle tool kit and inner tubes are recommended. The Peace Corps will provide a helmet

- Laptop computer—If you already own one, it may be worth bringing, as many Volunteers find it very helpful to have one. Conditions are hard on computers, but insurance is available. Most locations have electricity, though a small number of assignments are in locations that have electricity only at certain times or not at all

- Electrical converter for 220 volts (the same as Australia)

- External hard drive for easy computer information storage and transportation and to share media with other Volunteers

- Sunglasses

- Sun hat or visor

- Ear plugs

- Extra pair of glasses

- School supplies (e.g., highlighters, index cards, stapler and staples, glue sticks, rubber bands, paper, laminating sheets, etc.)

- Waterproof zippered plastic bags to help protect valuables and to keep clothes and important papers dry

- Hammock–for camping or for in your house

- Tent–if you plan on doing any camping

- Travel alarm clock

- World map–great for entertaining the local kids or teaching at schools

- Duct tape

- Games–anything you can pack easily, including a deck of cards

Don't bring anything made from leather, including shoes, belts, and wallets. They will attract mildew.

PRE-DEPARTURE CHECKLIST

The following list consists of suggestions for you to consider as you prepare to live outside the United States for two years. Not all items will be relevant to everyone, and the list does not include everything you should make arrangements for.

Family

- Notify family that they can call the Peace Corps' Counseling and Outreach Unit at any time if there is a critical illness or death of a family member (24-hour telephone number: 800.424.8580, extension 1470).

- Give the Peace Corps' *On the Home Front* handbook to family and friends.

Passport/Travel

- Forward to the Peace Corps travel office all paperwork for the Peace Corps passport and visas.

- Verify that your luggage meets the size and weight limits for international travel.

- Obtain a personal passport if you plan to travel after your service ends. (Your Peace Corps passport will expire three months after you finish your service, so if you plan to travel longer, you will need a regular passport.)

Medical/Health

- Complete any needed dental and medical work.

- If you wear glasses, bring two pairs.

- Arrange to bring a three-month supply of all medications (including birth control pills) you are currently taking.

Insurance

- Make arrangements to maintain life insurance coverage.

- Arrange to maintain supplemental health coverage while you are away. (Even though the Peace Corps is responsible for your health care during Peace Corps service overseas, it is advisable for people who have pre-existing conditions to arrange for the continuation of their supplemental health coverage. If there is a lapse in coverage, it is often difficult and expensive to be reinstated.)

- Arrange to continue Medicare coverage if applicable.

Personal Papers

- Bring a copy of your certificate of marriage or divorce.

Voting

- Register to vote in the state of your home of record. (Many state universities consider voting and payment of state taxes as evidence of residence in that state.)

- Obtain a voter registration card and take it with you overseas.

- Arrange to have an absentee ballot forwarded to you overseas.

Personal Effects

- Purchase personal property insurance to extend from the time you leave your home for service overseas until the time you complete your service and return to the United States.

Financial Management

- Keep a bank account in your name in the U.S.

- Obtain student loan deferment forms from the lender or loan service.

- Execute a Power of Attorney for the management of your property and business.

- Arrange for deductions from your readjustment allowance to pay alimony, child support, and other debts through the Office of Volunteer Financial Operations at 800.424.8580, extension 1770.

- Place all important papers—mortgages, deeds, stocks, and bonds—in a safe deposit box or with an attorney or other caretaker.

CONTACTING PEACE CORPS HEADQUARTERS

This list of numbers will help connect you with the appropriate office at Peace Corps headquarters to answer various questions. You can use the toll-free number and extension or dial directly using the local numbers provided. Be sure to leave the toll-free number and extensions with your family so they can contact you in the event of an emergency.

Peace Corps Headquarters Toll-free Number: 800.424.8580, Press 2, Press 1, then Ext. # (see below)

Peace Corps' Mailing Address: Peace Corps Headquarters
1111 20th Street, NW
Washington, DC 20526

For Questions About:	Staff:	Toll-Free Ext:	Direct/Local Number:
Responding to an Invitation:	Office of Placement	x1840	202.692.1840
Country Information:	Shelley Swendiman Desk Officer / Fiji, Samoa, Tonga sswendiman@peacecorps.gov	x2523	202.692.2523
	Sasha Cooper-Morrison Desk Officer / Micronesia, Palau, Vanuatu scoopermorrison@peacecorps.gov	x2502	202.692.2502
Plane Tickets, Passports, Visas, or other travel matters:			
	CWT SATO Travel	x1170	202.692.1170
Legal Clearance:	Office of Placement	x1840	202.692.1840
Medical Clearance and Forms Processing (includes dental):			
	Screening Nurse	x1500	202.692.1500
Medical Reimbursements (handled by a subcontractor):			800.818.8772

Loan Deferments, Taxes, Financial Operations: x1770   202.692.1770

Readjustment Allowance Withdrawals, Power of Attorney, Staging (Pre-Departure Orientation), and Reporting Instructions:

                Office of Staging   x1865   202.692.1865

Note: You will receive comprehensive information (hotel and flight arrangements) three to five weeks prior to departure. This information is not available sooner.

Family Emergencies (to get information to a Volunteer overseas) *24 hours:*

                Counseling &   x1470   202.692.1470

                Outreach Unit

www.ingramcontent.com/pod-product-compliance
Lightning Source LLC
Chambersburg PA
CBHW081759280526
45789CB00008B/2915